THE -'CIDES' OF KILLING
A DICTIONARY OF KILLING TERMS ENDING IN -'CIDE', AND THEIR MEANINGS

By:

Kevin R. Sweeter

Contents

Introduction — Page 1

A Terms — Page 3

B Terms — Page 9

C Terms — Page 11

D Terms — Page 15

E Terms — Page 17

F Terms — Page 19

G Terms — Page 23

H Terms — Page 27

I Terms — Page 31

J Terms — Page 33

L Terms — Page 35

M Terms — Page 39

N Terms — Page 45

O Terms — Page 47

P Terms — Page 49

R Terms   Page 55

S Terms   Page 57

T Terms   Page 63

U Terms   Page 69

V Terms   Page 71

W, X, & Z Terms   Page 73

Author's Note   Page 75

Introduction

Here is a collection of terms used to label types and means of death, killing, termination of life, and murder. There are terms that cover just about every facet of life and situation than end in 'cide', with a few exceptions such as mass-murder, and capital punishment.

A Terms

Aborticide:

- The act of destroying a fetus within the uterus

- An agent that destroys the fetus and causes abortion

- The killing of a fetus

- Abortion

Acaricide:

- A substance poisonous to mites or ticks

- A chemical agent used to kill mites

Adulticide:

- The killing of adult insects

- An insecticide used to kill adult insects

Ailurophileocide:

- The killing of a cat lover (Joke)

Algaecide:

- A chemical agent that kills algae

Ambicide:

- An antimicrobial that attacks more than one type of organism (such as both bacteria and protozoa)

Amebicide:

- An agent that is destructive to ameba

Amicicide:

- The act of killing a friend

Amoebicide:

- Is an agent used in the treatment of amoebozoa infections, called amoebiasis

Androcide:

- Refers to the systematic killing of men, boys, or males in general

Anophelicide:

- The killing of Mosquitos

- That which kills Mosquitoes

Anthracocide:

- Capable of destroying the bacteria of anthrax

Aphicide:

- An insecticide used against aphids

Aphidicide:

- A substance used to kill aphids

Apicide:

- Any substance used for killing bees

Apricide:

- The killing of boars

- A substance or agent that kills boars

Arachnidcide:

* A substance that kills arachnids (such as mites)

* The killing of spiders or scorpions

Arborcide:

* The deliberate killing of trees

Ascaricide:

* An agent or substance that kills Ascarids (Roundworms)

Autocide:

* The act of killing someone with a motor vehicle

* Suicide by automobile

Autoerotic asphyxiation:

* Suicide by accidental self-suffocation for sexual arousal

* A state of asphyxia intentionally induced (as by smothering or strangling oneself) so as to heighten sexual arousal during masturbation

Auto-ethnocide:

• The destruction of an ethnic culture by its own members

Avicide:

• A chemical agent that kills birds

• Is any substance (normally, a chemical) which can be used to kill birds. Commonly used Avicides include: Strychnine, DRC-1339 (3-chloro-4-methylaniline hydrochloride, Starlicide) and CPTH (3-chloro-p-toluidine, the free base of Starlicide), and Avitrol (4-aminopyridine)

Avunculicide:

• The act of killing an uncle

(The word can also refer to someone who commits such an act. The term is derived from the Latin words avunculus meaning "maternal uncle" and caedere meaning "to cut or kill". Edmunds suggests that in mythology avunculicide is a substitute for parricide)

B Terms

Bacillicide:

- Any material that kills bacilli bacteria

Bacteriacide:

- A substance that kills bacteria

Bactericide:

- Any drug that destroys bacteria or inhibits their growth

- A substance that kills bacteria

Biocide:

- A chemical agent that kills a broad spectrum of living organisms

- Killing living material

- A poisonous substance, especially a pesticide

- The destruction of life

Birdicide:

• The killing of birds

• The death of a bird by an intentional self-harming act

Bovicide:

• The killing of a cow

• One who kills cows

• The slaughter of cattle

• One who kills cattle, oxen, or any member of the bovine species

Brahmanicide:

• Killing a Brahmin

C Terms

Candicidin:

- An antibiotic obtained from a streptomyces (Streptomyces griseus) and active against some fungi of the genus Candida

Canicide:

- The killing of dogs

Capital punishment:

- The judicial killing of a human being for odious crimes

- The legally authorized killing of someone as punishment for a crime

Celebricide:

- The untimely death of a 'Celebrity' be it either be by suicide or Homicide

Cervicide:

- The act of killing deer

- Deer-slaying

Ceticide:

- The killing of whales and other cetaceans

Christicide:

- (rare, uncountable) The killing of Christ

- (rare) One responsible for the death of Christ

Chronocide:

- The killing of time (informal)

- The act of killing time

Cimicide:

- A substance used to kill bed-bugs

Computercide:

- The destruction of a computer

Copicide:

• A method of suicide in which a person deliberately behaves in a threatening manner to provoke a police officer into shooting them. (informal) The act of killing a police officer

Cosmocide:

• The ultimate death of the cosmos / universe (when all the stars have run out of nuclear fuel)

Cousinicide:

• (Informal) for the killing of a cousin (not officially recognized)

Culicide:

• A chemical agent that kills Mosquitos or Gnats

Culturcide:

• The systematic Destroying of cultural value on the basis of their ethnicity, religion, political beliefs, social status, or other particularities

Culturecide:

• Is referred to also as cultural genocide or deculturation, signifies processes that have usually been purposely introduced that result in the decline or demise of a culture, without necessarily resulting in the physical destruction of its bearers

Cybercide:

• Is a slang term for the deletion of an individual's entire online presences.

• Cybercide includes the removal of all social media profiles, shared photos, blog posts, directory entries and so on.

• Generally, a person commits cybercide out of a desire to be less connected and dependent on the Internet

Cytocide:

• An agent that is destructive to cells

Czaricide:

• The killing of a czar

• Alternative spelling of Tsaricide

D Terms

Deicide:

- The act of killing a god(s) or divine being(s)

Democide:

- The murder of any person or people by a government

Democracide:

- Is a term revived and redefined by the political scientist R. J. Rummel as "the murder of any person or people by their government, including genocide, politicide, and mass murder". ... Rummel explicitly excludes battle deaths in his definition

Dominicide:

- The act of killing one's master

E Terms

Ecocide:

• The destruction of the natural environment by such activity as war, overexploitation of resources, or pollution

Elephanticide:

• The act of or killing of elephants

Endectocide:

• A drug effective against both endoparasites and ectoparasites (for example, the macrolide antibiotic avermectin)

Episcopicide:

• The act of or killing of bishops

Epizocide:

• A chemical or agent used in the killing of Animal parasites

Ethnocide:

• The deliberate and systematic destruction of the culture of an ethnic group

Euthanasia (also mercy killing):

• The killing of any being for compassionate reasons, such as because of a significant injury or disease

F Terms

Facticide:

- The deliberate or intentional killing facts (distorting the truth)

- An effort to mislead using falsifications

Famacide:

- The killing or destroying of another's reputation

- A slander

Familiaricid:

- The act of killing a family for their property and/or possessions

Familicide:

- Is a multiple-victim homicide where a killer's spouse and children are slain

Febricide:

- Reducing or tending to reduce fever

- A medication that reduces fever

Felicide:

- The act of or the killing of cats

Femicide:

- The killing of a woman or girl, in particular by a man and on account of her gender

Feticide:

- The act of killing a fetus

- The destruction or abortion of a fetus

Fideicide:

- The destruction or killing a faith

Filaricide:

- An agent that is destructive to filariae

- (a threadlike parasitic nematode worm transmitted by biting flies and mosquitoes, causing filariasis and related diseases)

- (Roundworms)

Filicide:

- The act of a parent killing his or her son or daughter

Floricide:

- The deliberate killing of or the killer of flowers

Foeticide:

- The act of killing a fetus

- The destruction or abortion of a fetus

Formicide:

- A substance that kills ants

- The killing of ants

Fratricide:

• The act of killing a brother / sibling

• In military context, death by friendly fire

Fungicide:

• Chemical agents or biological organisms used to kill or inhibit fungi or fungal spores

G Terms

Gallicide:

- Killing of fowls

- The killing of a chicken, especially the former sport of cock-throwing

- (Humor) the killing of a Frenchman

Gallinicide:

- The killing of Chickens or Turkeys

Gametocide:

- To kill

- Any agent that is destructive to gametes or gametocytes

(The term is most often used to refer to agents specific for gametocytes of the protozoon Plasmodium, which causes malaria or malarial parasites)

Gendercide:

- The systematic killing of members of a specific sex or gender, either males, females, or non-binary

Genericide:

• Is a legal term for gentrification, the historical process whereby a brand name or trademark is transformed through popular usage into a common noun

Genocide:

• The systematic extermination of an entire national, racial, religious, or ethnic group

• The murder of any person or people by a government

Genticide:

• The killing of a race or nation of people; the slaughter of an ethnic group

• A genocide

Geocide:

• Earth-destruction (unofficial)

• The destruction of Earth (unofficial)

Geriatricide:

• The killing of elderly people

Germicide:

• An agent (as heat, radiation or a chemical) that destroys microorganisms that might carry disease

Geronticide:

• The abandonment of the elderly to die, commit suicide or be killed

Gerontocide:

• Alternate form of Geronticide

Giganticide:

• The act of or killing of a giant

Globulicide:

• An agent, which is destructive to the blood corpuscles

• Any older term for an erythrotoxic or erythrocidal substance such as hemolysin.

(It is not used in the working medical parlance)

Gonocide:

• An agent that kills the bacterium causing gonorrhea

Gynaecide:

• An obsolete term once used to describe the systematic killing of women

Gynecide:

• The systematic killing of women or a woman

Gynocide:

• The systematic killing of women or a woman

H Terms

Helminthicide:

- Any substance used to kill helminths

- A parasitic worm

- A fluke, tapeworm, or nematode Hepcidin:

Herbicide:

- A chemical agent that destroys plants or inhibits their growth

Hereticide:

- The Killing of heretics or a heretic

Heretocide:

- The Killing of heretics or a heretic

Hericide:

- The killing of a lord or master

Herpecide:

• The killing of reptiles

Herpicide:

• The killing of reptiles

Hiricide:

• The killing of goats

Hirudicide:

• The killing of leeches

Historicide:

• The murder of history; accomplished when a historian leans too far to the postmodernist/relativist or too far to the scientific/objectivist side of the spectrum

Homicide:

• The killing of a man, or any person, a human being by another human being

Honor killing:

• The act of killing a family member who has or was perceived to have brought disgrace to the family

Hospiticide:

• The act of a guest killing his host or vice versa, or an instance thereof

Hosticide:

• The killing an enemy

• One who kills an enemy

Human sacrifice:

• The killing of a human for sacrificial, often religious, reasons.

I Terms

Imagicide:

- The killing of adult insects; especially, mosquitoes

Imagocide:

- The killing of adult insects; especially, mosquitoes

Infanticide:

- The act of killing a child within the first year of its life

Insecticide:

- A chemical used to kill bugs

Involuntary Manslaughter:

- The crime of killing another human being unlawfully but unintentionally

J Terms

Jedicide:

- The systematic and planned extermination of members of the Jedi order

Judeocide:

- The killing of Jews

Justice:

- The killing of a mother-in-law (Joke)

L Terms

Lampricide:

• Is any chemical designed to target the larvae of lampreys in river systems before they develop into parasitic adults.

It is used in the headwaters of Lake Champlain and the Great Lakes to control sea lamprey (Petromyzon marinus), an invasive species to these lakes

Larvicide:

• An insecticide targeted against the larval life stage of an insect

Legicide:

• North American reference. The action or an act of destroying or undermining the authority of the law

• The act of defeating or preventing the passage of a particular piece of legislation

Leucocide:

• The killing of leukocytes (white blood corpuscles)

Liberticide:

• The destruction of liberty

• A destroyer of liberty

Licecide:

• (rare) A lousicide

• A substance that kills lice

Linguicide:

• Intentionally causing the death of a language

Logocide:

• Refers to the destruction or perversion of meaning, something deadly to reason and communication

• The Destruction of Language

Lousicide:

• A louse-killing insecticide

Lumbricide:

• A family of segmented worms containing most of the earthworms of Eurasia and North America

• Roundworms

Lupicide:

• The killing of wolves

Lupidide:

• The killing of wolves

M Terms

Macropocide:

- The killing of kangaroos

Magistricide:

- The killing of one's master or teacher. (rare)

- A person who kills their master or teacher

Malecide:

- The killing of evil

Manslaughter:

- Murder, but under legally mitigating factors.

Mariticide:

- Killing or the killer of one's husband

Mass Murder:

- The indiscriminate killing of any person or people by a government

Matricide:

• The killing of one's mother

Medicide:

• A suicide accomplished with the aid of a physician.

Memocide:

• An attempt to eradicate one or more ideas

(for example eradication by book burning and censorship)

Menticide:

• Reduction of mind by psychological pressure

• Killing the mind (brainwashing)

Mercy Killing:

• The killing of a patient suffering from an incurable and painful disease, typically by the administration of large doses of painkilling drugs

Microbicide:

• An agent used to kill or reduce the infectiousness of microorganisms.

Microbicide:

- The killing of or killer of microbes

Mildewcide:

- An agent that destroys mildew

Miticide:

- An agent that kills mites

Modernicide:

- The killing of a modernist

Molluscacide:

- The killing of snails / mollusks

Molluscicide:

- The killing of snails / mollusks

Monstricide:

- The killing of a monster

Mosquitocide:

• The killing of mosquitos

Multicide:

• The killing of multiple people

• Mass murder or serial killing

Mundicide:

• The Destruction of the entire world

Municide:

• The demise of a city through economic collapse or disincorporation

Murder:

• The malicious and unlawful killing of a human by another human.

Murder-suicide:

• A suicide committed immediately after one or more murders

Muricide:

• The killing of mice

Muscacide:

• The killing of flies

Muscicide:

• An agent that kills flies.

Mycocide:

• A fungicide that destroys molds

N Terms

Nanocide:

- Any pesticide created using nanotechnology

Nemacide:

- A substance used to kill nematode worms

Nemacide:

- A chemical to eradicate or kill nematodes.

Nematicide:

- A substance used to kill nematode worms

Nematicide:

- A substance used to kill nematode worms

Nematocide:

- A substance used to kill nematode worms

Neonaticide:

• The act of killing an infant within the first twenty-four hours or month (varies by individual and jurisdiction) of its life

Nepoticide:

• The killing of a nephew

• The word can also refer to someone who commits such an act.

O Terms

Omnicide:

- The act of killing all humans

- To create intentional extinction of the human species

- Destruction of everything

Ovacide:

- An agent that kills eggs of an organism particular a pest, such as lice eggs.

Ovicide:

- Sheep-killing

- The killing of Sheep

Oxyuricide:

- An agent that kills Oxyurida worms

- Kills any of the order Oxyurida of nematode worms

P Terms

Papicide:

- The act of killing the Pope

Parasiticide:

- A general term to describe an agent used to destroy parasites

Parasuicide:

- A harmful act appearing to be an attempt at suicide

Parenticide:

- A person who kills one or both of his or her parents

- The act of killing one's parent or parents

Parricide:

- The killing of one's mother, father, or other close relative

Patricide:

- The killing of one's father

Pediculicide:

- A chemical agent that kills lice

- An agent that kills head lice

Pediculicide:

- The killing of lice

Perdricide:

- The killing of partridges

Pesticide:

- A general term to describe an agent used to destroy or repel a pest

Petracide:

- The destruction of ancient buildings or monuments

Philosophicide:

- The killing of a philosopher

Phytocide:

- The killing of plants

Pilicide:

• Any of several substances that reduce the number of hair like Pili on the surface of bacteria and thus reduce its ability to adhere to human tissue

Piscicide:

• The killing of fish

Planetcide:

• The act of killing all living creatures on a planet

Plasmodicide:

• An agent used to kill malaria parasites

Policide:

• Is a neologism used in political science to describe the intentional destruction of a city or nation

Politicide:

• The murder of any person or people by a government because of their politics or for political purposes

Populicide:

- The slaughter of a people

- A massacre

Porcicide:

- The systematic killing off of pigs in large numbers

Poultrycide:

- The killing of poultry

Prenticecide:

- The killing of an apprentice

Prolicide:

- The killing of offspring

- The killing of the human race

Protozoacide:

- Destructive to, or that which kills, Protozoa, Protozoans

(Any of a large group of one-celled organisms called Protists that live in water or as parasites)

Pseudocide:

• A faked death, also called a pseudocide, is a case in which an individual leaves evidence to suggest that they are dead to mislead others

Pulicicide:

• An agent that kills fleas

Pulicide:

• A flea-killer

Patricide:

• The killing of one's father

R Terms

Raticide:

- An agent for killing rats.

Raticide:

- The killing of rats

Raticide:

- A substance or person who kills rats

Regicide:

- The killing of a monarch

Religicide:

- The destruction of a religion

Rodenticide:

- The killing of rodents

S Terms

Scabicide:

* A drug that destroys the itch mite that causes scabies

Scabieticide:

* A drug that destroys the itch mite that causes scabies

Schistosomicide:

* Any drug used to combat schistosomiasis

Schizonticide:

* An agent selectively destructive of the schizont of a sporozoan parasite

Scienticide:

* The destruction or debasement of scientific method, understanding, and/or infrastructure; a (figurative) killing of science

Sealicide:

* The killing of seals

Selfcide:

• Killing oneself

• Suicide

Self-immolation:

• Suicide by setting oneself on fire

• A form of extreme protest

Senicide:

• The killing of one's elderly family members when they can no longer work or become a burden

Serpenticide:

• The killing of or a killer of a snake

Siblicide:

• The killing of an infant individual by its close relatives (full or half siblings)

• The killing or killer of a sibling

Silicide:

• Any of various compounds of silicon with a more electropositive element or radical

Silvicide:

• A substance that kills trees

Slaughter:

• The killing of Animals for food

• To butcher

Sociocide:

• The destruction of a society

• Somebody who threatens society

Sororicide:

• The killing of one's own sister

Sparrowcide:

• The killing of sparrows

Sparticide:

• The killing of a Spartacus member

Speciocide:

• The destruction of an entire species

Spermatocide:

• A less common word for spermicide

Spermatozoicide:

• An agent that destroys spermatozoa

• A spermicide

Spermicide:

• A contraceptive agent to render sperm inert and prevent fertilization

Spirillicide:

• An agent that is destructive to Spirilla bacteria

Spirochaeticide:

• An agent such as a drug capable of killing Spirochetes bacteria especially within the human or animal body

Spirocheticide:

• An agent such as a drug capable of killing Spirochetes bacteria especially within the human or animal body

Sporicide:

• Tending to kill spores

• An agent that kills spores

Squirrelcide:

• (very rare) Squirrel suicide, often with connotations of taking human equipment with it

Staphylocide:

• Killing staphylococci

Staphylococcicide:

• Killing staphylococci

Staphylococcide:

• Killing staphylococci

Streptococcicide:

• **A** proteolytic enzyme produced by hemolytic streptococci that promotes the dissolution of blood clots by activating plasminogen to produce plasmin

Suicide:

• The intentional killing of self

Suicide by cop:

• Acting in a threatening manner so as to provoke a lethal response from law enforcement

Suitorcide:

• Ruining a suitor's chances

T Terms

Taeniacide:

- The killing of tapeworms

- An agent that destroys tapeworms

Taeniacide:

- A chemical agent that kills tape worms

Taenicide:

- A chemical agent that kills tape worms

Talpicide:

- The killing of moles

Tauricide:

- The killing of bulls or steers.

Technocide:

• The destruction of technology

Teniacide:

• A chemical agent that kills tape worms.

Tenicide:

• A chemical agent that kills tape worms.

Terracide:

• The destruction of a planet or of the natural ecosystems

Tickicide:

• The killing of ticks

Tomecide:

• The destruction of books

Toxicide:

• Destructive to toxins

• A chemical antidote for poisons

Toxinicide:

• That which is destructive to toxins

Treponemicide:

• An agent that kills Treponemata

(Any of a genus Treponema of spirochetes that are pathogenic in humans and other warm-blooded animals and include the causative agents of syphilis and yaws)

Trichomonacide:

• An agent used to destroy Trichomonads

(a parasitic protozoan with four to six flagella and an undulating membrane, infesting the urogenital or digestive system)

• A diarrhea-causing parasite

Trypanocide:

• An agent that kills trypanosomes

• Also called Trypanosomicide

(a single-celled parasitic protozoan with a trailing flagellum, infesting the blood)

• The killing of trypanosomes

• Sleeping sickness infection

Trypanocide:

• An agent that kills trypanosomes

• Also called Trypanosomicide

(a single-celled parasitic protozoan with a trailing flagellum, infesting the blood)

• The killing of trypanosomes

• Sleeping sickness infection

Trypanosomacide:

•Any of a genus Trypanosoma of parasitic flagellate protozoans that infest the blood of various vertebrates including humans, and are usually transmitted by the bite of an insect, and include some that cause serious diseases such as sleeping sickness and Chagas disease

• Sleeping sickness infection

Tsaricide:

• The killing of a Tsar

Tuberculocide:

• Any disinfectant certified by the U.S. Food and Drug Administration as having the ability to kill Mycobacterium tuberculosis as well as less resistant microorganisms such as other bacteria, viruses, and fungi

(A Tuberculocidal disinfectant is not certified to kill bacterial spores)

Tumorcide:

• Destroying tumor cells, tumoricidal activity, tumoricidal macrophages, cancerous cells

Tyrannicide:

• The killing of a tyrant

U Terms

Urbicide:

• The destruction of a city or the stifling of an urbanization

Ursicide:

• The killing or killer of a bear

Utricide:

• One who stabs an inflated skin vessel instead of killing someone

Uxoricide:

• Is one who commits uxoricide

• The killing of one's own wife

V Terms

Vaccicide:

• The killing of cows

Vaticide:

• The killing of a prophet or poet

Verbicide:

• Destroying the meaning of a word

Vermicide:

•An agent used to kill parasitic intestinal worms.

Verminicide:

• The killing of vermin

Vespacide:

• A chemical agent that kills wasps.

Vindication:

• The Killing of an ex-wife (Joke)

Viricide:

• An agent capable of destroying or inhibiting viruses.

Viricide:

• The killing of viruses

• The killing of men or of husbands

Virucide:

• An agent that inactivates or destroys viruses

Viruscide:

• An agent that inactivates or destroys viruses

Vulpicide:

• The killing of a fox by methods other than by hunting it with hounds

Vulpecide:

The killing of a fox by methods other than by hunting it
with hounds

W, X, & Z

Weedicide:

•Something that kills weeds

Xenocide:

• The genocide of an entire alien species

Zoocide:

• Any substance intended to kill animals

Author's Note:

I thank you for your patronage and hope that you enjoy your new book! Reviews are encouraged; please feel free to share your experience with others.

~Kevin R. Sweeter

Follow on my Amazon **Author Page: https://www.amazon.com/Kevin-R.Sweeter/e/B00500O7U4**

Keep up to date with availability and promotions.

Contact **E-mail**: **kevin.r.sweeter.author@gmail.com**

Please subscribe to my author email list for news, updates, and special offers and events.

Like, Follow, and Share on my **Facebook Author Page**:

https://www.facebook.com/Kevin-Sweeter-Author-209756967060/

Visit the book pages; see what is in the works, what is published, what will come soon, and what the books are about. Invite your friends to 'like' my pages.

www.ingramcontent.com/pod-product-compliance
Lightning Source LLC
Chambersburg PA
CBHW060757260726
48660CB00002B/663